KRISHNA MOHAN AVANCHA

Facebook: Lead generation

Contents

1

The Power of Facebook for Lead Generation

A s a digital marketer with years of experience in lead generation, I can confidently say that Facebook is one of the most powerful tools for generating leads in today's digital landscape. With over 2 billion monthly active users, Facebook offers an unprecedented reach for businesses of all sizes to connect with their target audience and convert them into leads.

One of the main advantages of using Facebook for lead generation is its ability to target specific demographics. Facebook's advertising platform allows you to target users based on age, gender, location, interests, behaviors, and more. This level of granularity ensures that your ads are shown only to those who are most likely to be interested in your product or service, maximizing your return on investment.

Another powerful tool for lead generation on Facebook is the use of lead magnets. A lead magnet is a valuable resource, such as an eBook, whitepaper, or free trial, that is offered to users in exchange for their contact information. By providing something of value to your audience, you can attract their attention and build trust, increasing the likelihood that they will convert into leads.

Facebook also offers a variety of ad formats that can be used for lead generation, including carousel ads, video ads, and messenger ads. Each format offers a unique way to showcase your product or service and capture the attention of potential leads.

In addition to paid advertising, Facebook groups can also be a powerful tool for generating leads. By creating or joining groups that are relevant to your business, you can connect with potential customers and build relationships that can lead to sales down the line.

To make the most of Facebook for lead generation, it's important to track your results and optimize your campaigns based on your findings. Facebook's ad platform offers robust analytics tools that allow you to track your ad performance and adjust your targeting and messaging accordingly.

In conclusion, Facebook is an incredibly powerful tool for lead generation, offering unparalleled reach and targeting capabilities. By leveraging the platform's advertising tools, lead magnets, groups, and analytics, businesses can connect with their target audience and convert them into valuable leads.

2

The Importance of Defining Your Target Audience

As a digital marketer with years of experience in the field, I cannot emphasize enough the importance of defining your target audience when creating a marketing strategy. Target audience refers to a specific group of people that you want to reach with your marketing efforts. It could be a particular demographic, age group, location, or interest group. Knowing your target audience is essential because it allows you to create a targeted and more effective marketing campaign.

Defining your target audience involves researching and understanding their needs, wants, pain points, and preferences. This knowledge helps you create a marketing message that resonates with them and motivates them to take action. Here are some reasons why defining your target audience is crucial:

• Helps you create a more focused marketing strategy

When you define your target audience, you can create a

marketing strategy that is focused on reaching them. Instead of trying to appeal to everyone, you can tailor your messaging and content to address the specific needs and interests of your target audience. This approach helps you connect with your audience more effectively and generates better results.

- Saves time and resources

Without a defined target audience, your marketing efforts may be scattered and ineffective. You may waste time and resources on marketing channels that don't reach your audience, resulting in low ROI. Defining your target audience helps you focus your efforts and allocate resources more efficiently.

- Increases the effectiveness of your messaging

When you know your target audience, you can craft messaging that speaks directly to them. You can use language and tone that resonates with them and addresses their pain points. This approach makes your messaging more effective and helps you build a stronger connection with your audience.

- Helps you create products and services that meet their needs

Understanding your target audience helps you create products and services that meet their needs. By conducting research and collecting data, you can identify gaps in the market and create solutions that address their pain points. This approach helps you build a more loyal customer base and generates more revenue.

In conclusion, defining your target audience is essential for creating a successful marketing strategy. It helps you focus your efforts, allocate resources efficiently, create more effective messaging, and develop products and services that meet their needs. If you haven't defined your target audience yet, it's time to start now. Conduct research, gather data, and use the insights to create a marketing strategy that resonates with your audience and generates better results.

3

How to Create a Facebook Business Page that Attracts Leads

C reating a Facebook business page is an essential step for any company that wants to establish an online presence and attract potential customers. However, simply creating a page is not enough. You need to make sure that it is designed in a way that appeals to your target audience and encourages them to engage with your business.

Here are some tips on how to create a Facebook business page that attracts leads:

- Choose a relevant profile picture and cover photo

Your profile picture and cover photo are the first things visitors see when they come to your page. Make sure they are relevant and eye-catching. Your profile picture should be your company logo, and your cover photo should showcase your product or service.

- Optimize your About section

Your About section is an opportunity to provide visitors with more information about your business. Make sure you include a brief description of your company, your mission statement, and your contact information. You can also add a call-to-action button that directs visitors to your website or a specific landing page.

- Post engaging content

Posting engaging content is essential for attracting and retaining visitors to your page. Share news, updates, promotions, and other relevant information that your target audience will find interesting. Make sure you include images, videos, and infographics to make your content more visually appealing.

- Use Facebook Ads

Facebook Ads are an effective way to reach your target audience and attract leads to your business page. You can use Facebook's targeting options to select specific demographics, interests, and behaviors to ensure that your ads reach the right people. Make sure you have a clear call-to-action in your ad that directs visitors to your page.

- Engage with your followers

Engaging with your followers is essential for building relationships and establishing trust with your audience. Respond to comments, messages, and reviews promptly and professionally. You can also use Facebook Live to interact with your followers in real-time and answer any questions they may have.

- Measure your results

Measuring your results is essential for evaluating the effectiveness of your Facebook page and making improvements where necessary. Facebook Insights provides data on your page's performance, including engagement, reach, and audience demographics. Use this data to adjust your content strategy and optimize your page for maximum results.

In conclusion, creating a Facebook business page that attracts leads requires careful planning and execution. By following these tips, you can create a page that engages your target audience and encourages them to take action. Remember to continually monitor and adjust your strategy to ensure that you are getting the best results possible.

4

Crafting a Winning Lead Magnet Strategy on Facebook

As a digital marketer with extensive experience in crafting successful lead magnet strategies on Facebook, I can tell you that having a well-thought-out approach is essential to achieving your goals. A lead magnet is a free offer that you give to your target audience in exchange for their contact information, such as their email address. The purpose of a lead magnet is to build your email list, which is an essential component of any digital marketing campaign.

Here are some steps to help you craft a winning lead magnet strategy on Facebook:

- Define Your Target Audience

The first step in creating a successful lead magnet strategy is to define your target audience. This means understanding who your ideal customer is, their pain points, and what they are looking for in a solution. Once you have a clear understanding of your target audience, you can create a lead magnet that speaks directly to their needs and interests.

• Choose a Relevant Lead Magnet

Your lead magnet should be relevant to your target audience and provide value. It should be something that your audience wants and needs. For example, if you're targeting small business owners, your lead magnet could be a guide to social media marketing for small businesses.

• Create a Landing Page

Once you have your lead magnet, you need to create a landing page where people can sign up to receive it. The landing page should be designed to convert visitors into leads, so make sure it's clear, concise, and visually appealing. The page should also include a form for visitors to fill out with their contact information.

• Drive Traffic to Your Landing Page

To get people to your landing page, you need to drive traffic to it. Facebook is an excellent platform for this as it has a vast user base and powerful targeting options. You can run Facebook ads, post on your Facebook page, and share your lead magnet in relevant Facebook groups.

• Follow-Up with Your Leads

Once you've collected leads, it's essential to follow up with them. Send them a welcome email, and then continue to provide them with valuable content through email marketing. This will help build a relationship with your leads and keep them engaged with your brand.

- Track Your Results

Finally, track your results to see how your lead magnet strategy is performing. Use tools like Google Analytics and Facebook Insights to measure your success. Look at metrics such as conversion rates, click-through rates, and email open rates to see what's working and what's not.

In conclusion, crafting a winning lead magnet strategy on Facebook requires careful planning, targeting, and execution. By following the steps outlined above, you can create a lead magnet that resonates with your target audience, drives traffic to your landing page, and ultimately builds your email list. Remember to track your results and make adjustments as needed to ensure your lead magnet strategy is a success.

5

Creating Effective Facebook Ads for Lead Generation

As a digital marketer with years of experience in creating effective Facebook ads for lead generation, I understand the importance of having a strategic approach when it comes to Facebook advertising. With over 2.8 billion monthly active users, Facebook is undoubtedly one of the most effective platforms for lead generation. However, creating effective Facebook ads requires a thorough understanding of your target audience, their pain points, and the right messaging to address those pain points.

Here are some tips to create effective Facebook ads for lead generation:

- Identify Your Target Audience

The first step in creating effective Facebook ads is to identify your target audience. Who are they? What are their interests? What are their pain points? Answering these questions will help you create ads that are relevant and engaging to your audience. You can use Facebook Audience Insights to get more information about your target audience, including their demographics, interests, and behaviors.

• Create a Compelling Offer

Once you have identified your target audience, the next step is to create a compelling offer that will entice them to take action. Your offer should be aligned with your audience's pain points and provide a solution to their problems. For example, if your target audience is struggling with weight loss, your offer could be a free e-book on healthy eating habits.

• Use Attention-Grabbing Images

Facebook is a visual platform, so it's essential to use attention-grabbing images that will capture your audience's attention. Your images should be relevant to your offer and convey the benefits of taking action. Avoid using generic stock photos and opt for custom images that showcase your brand's personality.

• Write Persuasive Ad Copy

Your ad copy should be persuasive and convey the benefits of your offer. Use emotional triggers to connect with your audience and address their pain points. Use strong headlines and subheadings to break up your copy and make it more readable. Keep your copy concise and focused on the benefits of taking action.

• Use Social Proof

Social proof is a powerful way to increase the credibility of your offer. Include customer testimonials or reviews in your ads to showcase how your product or service has helped others. This will help build trust with your audience and increase the likelihood of them taking action.

- Use a Strong Call-to-Action

Your call-to-action (CTA) is the most critical part of your ad. It tells your audience what action you want them to take and should be clear and concise. Use action-oriented language and create a sense of urgency to encourage your audience to take action.

- Test and Optimize Your Ads

Creating effective Facebook ads for lead generation is an ongoing process. It's essential to test and optimize your ads to ensure they are performing at their best. Test different images, ad copy, and CTAs to see what resonates with your audience. Use Facebook's ad manager to track your results and make data-driven decisions to optimize your ads.

In conclusion, creating effective Facebook ads for lead generation requires a strategic approach. By identifying your target audience, creating a compelling offer, using attention-grabbing images, writing persuasive ad copy, using social proof, using a strong call-to-action, and testing and optimizing your ads, you can create ads that will generate leads and grow your business.

6

Leveraging Facebook Groups to Generate Leads

F acebook Groups have emerged as a powerful tool for businesses and digital marketers to generate leads and reach out to their target audience. With more than 2.8 billion active users on Facebook, it is the world's largest social media platform, and Facebook Groups have become a valuable resource for businesses looking to connect with potential customers.

In this article, we will explore the ways in which digital marketers can leverage Facebook Groups to generate leads for their businesses.

• Join Relevant Groups

The first step to leveraging Facebook Groups is to find and join relevant groups related to your business niche. This can be done by using Facebook's search function and filtering the results based on keywords and location. Joining groups that are relevant to your industry and niche will give you access to a community of potential customers who are interested in your products or services.

- Build Relationships

Once you have joined relevant groups, the next step is to build relationships with the members. It is important to remember that Facebook Groups are not a platform for self-promotion, but rather a space to connect and engage with others. By engaging in conversations and providing value to the group, you can establish yourself as an authority in your field and gain the trust of potential customers.

- Share Valuable Content

Sharing valuable content in Facebook Groups can help you to establish yourself as a thought leader in your industry. By providing helpful tips and insights related to your niche, you can position yourself as an expert and gain the attention of potential customers. You can share blog posts, videos, infographics, and other types of content that provide value to the group.

- Offer Freebies

Offering freebies is another effective way to generate leads through Facebook Groups. This can include free e-books, webinars, and other resources that provide value to the group. By offering something of value for free, you can attract potential customers and build trust with them.

- Engage in Direct Messaging

Engaging in direct messaging is a great way to build relationships and generate leads through Facebook Groups. Once you have established yourself as an authority in your field, you can reach out to potential customers through direct messaging and offer your products or services. It is important to keep in mind that direct messaging should be used sparingly and only with those who have expressed interest in your business.

- Use Facebook Ads

Facebook Ads can be a powerful tool for generating leads through Facebook Groups. By targeting your ads to specific groups related to your niche, you can reach potential customers who are interested in your products or services. Facebook Ads can be targeted based on interests, demographics, and behavior, making it easy to reach your target audience.

In conclusion, Facebook Groups can be a valuable resource for digital marketers looking to generate leads and reach out to potential customers. By joining relevant groups, building relationships, sharing valuable content, offering freebies, engaging in direct messaging, and using Facebook Ads, you can leverage Facebook Groups to grow your business and reach your target audience.

7

The Dos and Don'ts of Running Facebook Contests for Lead Generation

F acebook contests can be a great way to generate leads for your business, but they can also be a source of frustration and wasted resources if not executed properly. As an experienced digital marketer, I have seen both the successes and failures of Facebook contests, and in this article, I will be sharing with you the dos and don'ts of running Facebook contests for lead generation.

Dos:

1. Set Clear Goals and Objectives: Before running any Facebook contest, it is crucial to identify your goals and objectives. What do you want to achieve from this contest? Is it to generate leads, increase engagement, or build brand awareness? Defining your goals and objectives will help you design your contest in a way that aligns with your business goals and ensures the success of your campaign.

2. Choose the Right Type of Contest: There are many different types of Facebook contests you can run, including sweepstakes, photo contests, caption contests, and more. It's important to choose the right type of contest that aligns with your business goals and target audience. For example, if your goal is to generate leads, a sweepstakes contest that requires participants to fill out a form with their contact information may be the best option.

3. Follow Facebook's Rules and Guidelines: Facebook has strict rules and guidelines when it comes to running contests on their platform. It's important to read and follow these rules to avoid having your contest taken down or your account suspended. Some of these rules include disclosing that Facebook is not responsible for the contest, not using Facebook features as a way to enter the contest, and not asking participants to share the contest on their personal timelines as a way to enter.

4. Promote Your Contest: A Facebook contest won't be successful if nobody knows about it. Promote your contest on your website, social media channels, email list, and any other relevant platforms. Utilize Facebook ads to reach a wider audience and drive more traffic to your contest.

5. Follow Up with Leads: After the contest has ended, make sure to follow up with the leads you generated. Send them a thank you email and provide them with more information about your business and how you can help them. This will help to nurture these leads and turn them into paying customers.

Don'ts:

1. Make It Too Complicated: A complicated contest will only discourage people from participating. Keep your contest simple and easy to enter. Don't require participants to jump through too many hoops, such as creating a video or writing a long essay. The easier it is to enter, the more likely people will participate.

2. Ignore Your Target Audience: Your contest should be designed with your target audience in mind. If you're targeting a younger demographic, a photo or video contest may be more effective than a text-based contest. Make sure to tailor your contest to your target audience to ensure the highest level of engagement.

3. Use False Advertising: Don't promise something in your contest that you can't deliver. This will only lead to disappointment and distrust among your audience. Make sure that the prize you're offering is something that you can realistically provide.

4. Neglect Legal Requirements: Running a Facebook contest may require you to follow certain legal requirements depending on your country or state. Make sure to do your research and comply with any legal regulations, such as registering your contest with the appropriate authorities or paying any necessary taxes.

5. Forget to Analyze Results: After your contest has ended, make sure to analyze the results. Did you achieve your goals and objectives? How many leads did you generate? What was the ROI of your contest? Analyzing these results will help you to identify what worked and what didn't, and make improvements for future contests.

8

Maximizing Your Lead Generation Efforts with Facebook Messenger

As a digital marketer with extensive experience in lead generation, I can confidently say that Facebook Messenger is one of the most effective tools for capturing leads and converting them into loyal customers. With over 2.8 billion active users, Facebook Messenger provides an incredible opportunity for businesses to connect with potential customers and build lasting relationships with them.

Here are some effective strategies that can help maximize your lead generation efforts with Facebook Messenger:

1. Use Messenger Bots: Messenger bots are AI-powered tools that can help automate your conversations with potential customers. By using bots, you can quickly respond to inquiries, provide relevant information, and capture leads even when you're not online. You can set up bots to answer frequently asked questions, qualify leads, and schedule appointments, among other things. Bots are particularly useful for businesses that receive a high

volume of inquiries and want to save time and resources.

2. Personalize your messages: Personalization is key to building strong relationships with potential customers. Use the customer's name and any other relevant information you have to make your messages more engaging and personalized. When you personalize your messages, you show your customers that you care about them and understand their needs, which can help build trust and loyalty.

3. Use lead magnets: A lead magnet is an incentive that you offer potential customers in exchange for their contact information. This could be anything from a free e-book or webinar to a discount or coupon code. By offering something of value, you can encourage potential customers to provide their contact information and become leads.

4. Run Facebook Messenger Ads: Facebook Messenger ads are a powerful way to reach potential customers and generate leads. Messenger ads are displayed in the user's Messenger inbox, making them highly visible and engaging. You can use Messenger ads to promote your lead magnets or offer free trials or consultations. Make sure your ads are targeted to the right audience to maximize their effectiveness.

5. Follow up with leads: Following up with leads is crucial for converting them into loyal customers. Use Messenger to send personalized follow-up messages and nurture your leads. You can send helpful resources, answer any questions they may have, and offer exclusive deals to keep them engaged and interested.

In conclusion, Facebook Messenger is a powerful tool for lead generation, but it's important to use it strategically to maximize its effectiveness. By using bots, personalizing your messages, offering lead magnets, running Messenger ads, and following up with leads, you can build strong relationships with potential customers and turn them into loyal customers.

9

Using Facebook Live to Drive Lead Generation

F acebook Live is a powerful tool that digital marketers can use to drive lead generation. With the rise of video content consumption and the need for personalized experiences, Facebook Live provides an opportunity for businesses to connect with their target audience in real-time, and generate leads in a unique and engaging way.

Here are some key strategies for using Facebook Live to drive lead generation:

1. Plan your content: Before you go live, plan out your content and prepare your messaging. It's important to have a clear goal and message in mind for your Facebook Live session. This will help you stay on track and deliver a valuable experience for your audience.

2. Promote your Facebook Live session: To generate leads, you need to get the word out about your Facebook Live session. Promote it on your social media channels, website, and email list. You can even consider running Facebook

Ads to target your ideal audience and drive more viewers to your session.

3. Create a compelling hook: When promoting your Facebook Live session, make sure to create a compelling hook that will entice your audience to tune in. This could be a special guest, a new product launch, or a limited-time offer.

4. Engage with your audience: During your Facebook Live session, engage with your audience by answering their questions and responding to comments. This will help build a relationship with your audience and establish trust.

5. Offer a lead magnet: To generate leads during your Facebook Live session, offer a lead magnet, such as a free e-book, webinar, or consultation. Make sure to promote the lead magnet throughout the session and provide clear instructions on how to sign up.

6. Follow up with leads: After your Facebook Live session, follow up with leads by sending them a personalized email or message. This is a crucial step in converting your leads into customers.

7. Analyze your results: To improve your future Facebook Live sessions, analyze your results and identify what worked well and what could be improved. This will help you optimize your strategy and drive even more leads in the future.

In conclusion, Facebook Live is a powerful tool that digital marketers can use to drive lead generation. By planning your content, promoting your session, engaging with your audience, offering a lead magnet, following up with leads, and analyzing your results, you can generate high-quality leads and build strong relationships with your target audience.

10

Creating a Facebook Lead Generation Funnel that Converts

Facebook has become one of the most effective digital marketing platforms for businesses of all sizes. With over 2.8 billion active users, Facebook offers an enormous potential for generating leads and driving sales. However, creating a Facebook lead generation funnel that converts requires a strategic approach and a deep understanding of your target audience. In this article, I will discuss the essential steps involved in creating a Facebook lead generation funnel that converts.

Step 1: Define your target audience

The first step in creating a successful Facebook lead generation funnel is to define your target audience. You need to have a clear understanding of who your ideal customer is and what their needs and preferences are. Use Facebook Insights and other social media analytics tools to gather data on your target audience's demographics, interests, and behaviors. This information will help you create targeted ads that speak directly to your audience's needs and interests.

Step 2: Develop a lead magnet

A lead magnet is a valuable piece of content that you offer in exchange for your audience's contact information, such as their email address. Your lead magnet could be an e-book, a white paper, a webinar, or any other content that your audience finds valuable. Make sure your lead magnet is relevant to your target audience and provides genuine value. Your lead magnet should be compelling enough to motivate your audience to take action.

Step 3: Create a Facebook ad campaign

Once you have defined your target audience and developed a lead magnet, you need to create a Facebook ad campaign. Your ad campaign should include a series of targeted ads that promote your lead magnet and encourage your audience to provide their contact information. Make sure your ad copy and images are attention-grabbing and compelling. Use Facebook's targeting options to reach your ideal audience and maximize the effectiveness of your ad campaign.

Step 4: Build a landing page

Your landing page is the web page that your audience lands on after clicking on your Facebook ad. Your landing page should be optimized for conversions and designed to encourage your audience to provide their contact information. Keep your landing page simple and focused on your lead magnet's benefits. Use clear and concise headlines, bullet points, and images to convey the value of your lead magnet.

Step 5: Implement a lead capture form

To capture your audience's contact information, you need to implement a lead capture form on your landing page. Your lead capture form should be simple and easy to fill out, with fields for your audience's name, email address, and any other relevant information. Use an eye-catching button that encourages your audience to submit their information.

Step 6: Follow up with leads

Once you have captured your audience's contact information, you need to follow up with them to nurture the relationship and convert them into paying customers. Use an email marketing automation tool to send personalized emails to your leads, offering them more valuable content and promoting your products or services. Make sure your emails are relevant and valuable to your audience, and always include a clear call to action.

In conclusion, creating a Facebook lead generation funnel that converts requires a strategic approach and a deep understanding of your target audience. By following the six essential steps outlined in this article, you can create a successful Facebook lead generation funnel that generates high-quality leads and drives sales for your business. Remember to always test and optimize your funnel to maximize its effectiveness and achieve your marketing goals.

11

The Role of Facebook Pixel in Lead Generation

As a digital marketer with vast experience in lead generation, I can attest to the fact that Facebook Pixel is an essential tool that can significantly boost lead generation efforts.

For those who may not know, Facebook Pixel is a tracking code that helps businesses track user behavior on their website. By installing Facebook Pixel on your website, you can gather valuable insights into your website visitors, including their interests, behavior, and demographics. With this information, you can optimize your website and create highly targeted ad campaigns to increase your chances of converting website visitors into leads.

Here's how Facebook Pixel works in lead generation:

• Custom Audience Creation

One of the key benefits of Facebook Pixel is that it enables businesses to create custom audiences based on website visitors' behavior. For instance, you can create an audience of people who visited a particular product page or added an item to their cart but did not complete the purchase. This audience can then be targeted with highly specific ads that aim to address the reasons why they didn't convert.

• Retargeting

Retargeting is another powerful way that Facebook Pixel can help businesses generate leads. By tracking user behavior on your website, Facebook Pixel can help you retarget people who have interacted with your website before but didn't convert. This means you can show highly targeted ads to people who have already shown an interest in your business, increasing the likelihood of them converting into leads.

• Lookalike Audience Creation

Another benefit of Facebook Pixel is that it can help businesses create lookalike audiences based on website visitors. Lookalike audiences are groups of people who share similar characteristics to your website visitors, such as demographics, interests, and behavior. By creating a lookalike audience, you can expand your reach and target people who are more likely to be interested in your business and therefore, generate more leads.

• Conversion Tracking

Finally, Facebook Pixel can help businesses track conversions on their website. By setting up conversion tracking, you can monitor which ads are generating the most leads and adjust your campaigns accordingly. This means you can allocate your marketing budget to the most effective campaigns, maximizing your lead generation efforts.

In conclusion, Facebook Pixel is a powerful tool that can significantly enhance lead generation efforts. By using it to track user behavior on your website, you can create highly targeted ads, retarget people who have already shown an interest in your business, expand your reach through lookalike audiences, and track conversions to optimize your campaigns. If you're not already using Facebook Pixel in your lead generation efforts, you're missing out on a valuable opportunity to generate more leads for your business.

The Art of Writing Facebook Ad Copy that Converts

As a digital marketer with years of experience in crafting Facebook ad copy that converts, I can tell you that it's not just about putting words together. It's an art that requires a deep understanding of your audience, their needs, and how your product or service can help solve their problems.

Here are some key principles and tips to keep in mind when writing Facebook ad copy that converts:

1. Know your audience: Before you start writing your ad copy, you need to know your target audience inside out. Understand their pain points, what motivates them, and what kind of language they use. This will help you craft copy that speaks directly to their needs and desires.

2. Focus on benefits, not features: Instead of just listing the features of your product or service, focus on how it can benefit your audience. For example, instead of saying "Our shoes have a durable sole," say "Our shoes will keep your feet comfortable all day long."

3. Use attention-grabbing headlines: Your headline is the first thing your audience will see, so it's essential to make it attention-grabbing. Use power words, questions, or intriguing statements to entice your audience to read on.

4. Keep it short and sweet: Facebook ads have limited space, so you need to get your message across quickly and concisely. Stick to short sentences and avoid using complex words or jargon.

5. Create a sense of urgency: Use language that creates a sense of urgency and encourages your audience to take action. For example, "Limited time offer" or "Sale ends soon" can motivate your audience to act quickly.

6. Use social proof: People are more likely to trust and buy from a company that has social proof, such as customer reviews or testimonials. Incorporate social proof into your ad copy to build trust with your audience.

7. A/B test your ad copy: To find out what works best for your audience, A/B test different variations of your ad copy. This will help you determine which copy resonates best with your audience and drives the most conversions.

In summary, writing Facebook ad copy that converts requires a deep understanding of your audience, a focus on benefits rather than features, attention-grabbing headlines, concise language, a sense of urgency, social proof, and A/B testing. With these principles and tips in mind, you can create ad copy that resonates with your audience and drives conversions for your business.

13

Advanced Targeting Strategies for Facebook Lead Generation

As a seasoned digital marketer, I have found that Facebook has become an increasingly important platform for lead generation, thanks to its advanced targeting capabilities. By utilizing the following advanced targeting strategies, you can effectively reach your target audience, generate high-quality leads, and improve your overall ROI.

1. Lookalike Audiences: Facebook's Lookalike Audiences feature allows you to target users who share similar characteristics to your existing customers. To create a Lookalike Audience, you simply upload a list of your existing customer data, and Facebook will use its algorithms to find users who share similar demographics, interests, and behaviors. By targeting users who are more likely to convert, you can improve your lead generation efforts.

2. Custom Audiences: Facebook's Custom Audiences feature enables you to target users who have already engaged with

your brand in some way, such as by visiting your website, filling out a form, or interacting with your content on Facebook. By targeting users who have already shown an interest in your brand, you can improve the effectiveness of your lead generation efforts.

3. Interest-Based Targeting: Facebook's Interest-Based Targeting feature allows you to target users based on their interests and hobbies. By targeting users who have expressed an interest in topics related to your brand, you can improve the relevance of your ads and increase your chances of generating high-quality leads.

4. Behavioral Targeting: Facebook's Behavioral Targeting feature allows you to target users based on their behaviors, such as their purchase history, device usage, and travel habits. By targeting users based on their behaviors, you can create highly targeted campaigns that are more likely to generate leads.

5. Retargeting: Facebook's Retargeting feature enables you to target users who have already interacted with your brand in some way, such as by visiting your website or viewing a product page. By retargeting these users with relevant ads, you can increase the likelihood of converting them into leads.

6. Demographic Targeting: Facebook's Demographic Targeting feature allows you to target users based on their age, gender, education, income, and other demographic factors. By targeting users who match your ideal customer profile, you can create highly effective campaigns that are more likely to generate leads.

7. Location-Based Targeting: Facebook's Location-Based Targeting feature allows you to target users based on

their geographic location. By targeting users in specific geographic locations, you can improve the relevance of your ads and increase the chances of generating leads in those areas.

In conclusion, Facebook's advanced targeting strategies provide digital marketers with a range of effective options to generate high-quality leads. By utilizing these strategies, you can improve the relevance of your ads, reach your target audience, and generate a higher ROI for your campaigns. So, take advantage of these targeting features and start generating more leads for your business today!

14

Nurturing Facebook Leads with Email Marketing

As a digital marketer, I have seen firsthand the power of combining social media and email marketing to nurture leads and convert them into loyal customers. In this article, we will explore the best practices for nurturing Facebook leads with email marketing.

- Create a Facebook lead generation campaign

The first step in nurturing Facebook leads with email marketing is to create a Facebook lead generation campaign. This involves creating an ad that offers something of value to your target audience, such as a free eBook, webinar, or consultation. When someone clicks on your ad, they will be directed to a landing page where they can provide their contact information in exchange for the offer.

- Segment your leads

Once you have captured leads through your Facebook lead generation campaign, it's important to segment them based on their interests and behaviors. This will enable you to send targeted and personalized email campaigns that are more likely to resonate with your audience.

For example, if someone has downloaded an eBook on social media marketing, you can segment them into a group of leads interested in social media. Then, you can send them a series of emails that provide more valuable content on social media marketing, such as blog posts, case studies, and infographics.

- Send a welcome email

After someone has provided their contact information through your Facebook lead generation campaign, it's important to send a welcome email. This email should thank them for their interest and provide them with the offer they signed up for. It's also a good idea to introduce your brand and let them know what they can expect from your email communications.

- Provide value with your email content

To nurture your Facebook leads, it's important to provide them with valuable and relevant content. This can include blog posts, case studies, industry news, and tips and tricks related to your products or services. The goal is to keep your leads engaged and interested in your brand, so they are more likely to convert into customers.

- Use automation to save time

One of the benefits of email marketing is that it can be automated, which saves time and resources. You can set up automated email campaigns that are triggered by specific actions, such as when someone downloads an eBook or abandons their cart on your website. This allows you to stay in touch with your leads without having to manually send each email.

- Include calls-to-action (CTAs)

Finally, it's important to include clear and compelling calls-to-action (CTAs) in your email communications. CTAs encourage your leads to take a specific action, such as visiting your website, signing up for a free trial, or making a purchase. Make sure your CTAs are prominent and relevant to the content of your emails.

In conclusion, nurturing Facebook leads with email marketing is a powerful strategy for converting leads into loyal customers. By creating targeted and personalized email campaigns, providing value with your content, and using automation to save time, you can build strong relationships with your leads and increase your chances of conversion.

15

Measuring the Success of Your Facebook Lead Generation Campaign

As a digital marketer, I understand the importance of generating leads through social media platforms like Facebook. However, generating leads is just the first step in the sales funnel. The success of your Facebook lead generation campaign is determined by how effectively you measure and analyze the data collected during the campaign. In this article, I'll discuss the various metrics and tools you can use to measure the success of your Facebook lead generation campaign.

1. Set Clear Goals: The first step in measuring the success of your Facebook lead generation campaign is to define clear and specific goals. What do you want to achieve with this campaign? Is it more website traffic, more leads, or increased brand awareness? Once you have set your goals, you can measure the success of your campaign based on how well you have achieved those goals.

2. Measure Engagement: One way to measure the success of

your Facebook lead generation campaign is to track the engagement of your target audience. Engagement metrics include likes, comments, shares, and click-through rates. If your engagement metrics are high, it indicates that your target audience is interested in your content and are likely to convert into leads.

3. Track Conversions: Conversions are the ultimate goal of any lead generation campaign. Conversions can be measured by tracking the number of people who completed your desired action after clicking on your ad, such as filling out a form, subscribing to a newsletter, or purchasing a product. Facebook's Ads Manager has a built-in conversion tracking tool that allows you to track the number of conversions your campaign has generated.

4. Analyze Your Landing Page: Your landing page is a critical element of your Facebook lead generation campaign. The landing page should be designed to convert visitors into leads by providing them with valuable information and a clear call-to-action. Analyze your landing page to see if it's optimized for conversions. Use A/B testing to test different variations of your landing page to see which one performs better.

5. Use Facebook Pixel: Facebook Pixel is a powerful tool that allows you to track the actions of people who visit your website after clicking on your Facebook ad. By using Facebook Pixel, you can track the behavior of your target audience and optimize your Facebook lead generation campaign accordingly.

6. Monitor Cost-Per-Lead: Cost-per-lead (CPL) is the amount of money you spend to acquire a single lead. Monitoring your CPL allows you to optimize your

campaign and reduce your acquisition costs. You can track your CPL using Facebook's Ads Manager.

7. Analyze ROI: Return on investment (ROI) is a crucial metric for measuring the success of any marketing campaign. Analyze the ROI of your Facebook lead generation campaign by comparing the amount of money you spent on the campaign to the revenue generated from the leads generated by the campaign.

In conclusion, measuring the success of your Facebook lead generation campaign requires careful planning, tracking, and analysis of various metrics. By setting clear goals, measuring engagement, tracking conversions, analyzing your landing page, using Facebook Pixel, monitoring cost-per-lead, and analyzing ROI, you can optimize your campaign for success and generate high-quality leads for your business.

16

Common Mistakes to Avoid in Facebook Lead Generation

As a digital marketer with extensive experience in Facebook lead generation, I have witnessed numerous businesses making the same mistakes repeatedly. These mistakes can have a significant impact on the success of your Facebook lead generation campaigns. Therefore, it is essential to be aware of them and take necessary measures to avoid them.

Here are some common mistakes to avoid in Facebook lead generation:

• Poorly defined audience targeting

One of the most common mistakes businesses make when running Facebook lead generation campaigns is failing to define their target audience correctly. It is crucial to identify your audience's demographics, interests, behaviors, and location to create effective ad campaigns that convert.

- Unclear Call-to-Action (CTA)

A clear and compelling call-to-action is essential to encourage users to take the desired action. Ensure that your CTA is concise, visible, and directs users to take the desired action. Without a clear CTA, your ads will not generate leads as you expect.

- Overcomplicating the Lead Form

Your lead form should be easy to fill out, clear, and concise. Overcomplicating your lead form with too many questions can lead to abandonment and deter users from providing their contact details. Keep it simple and ensure the form is mobile-responsive.

- Poor Landing Page Experience

Your landing page is critical in converting leads. Ensure that it is relevant, easy to navigate, and loads quickly. A poorly designed or slow landing page will cause users to abandon the page, leading to a high bounce rate and a low conversion rate.

- Ignoring Facebook Pixel

The Facebook pixel is an essential tool that tracks the actions of users on your website, allowing you to retarget them later. Ignoring the pixel can lead to missed opportunities to re-engage potential leads, and you won't be able to track your ad campaigns' success accurately.

- Neglecting Ad Testing

A/B testing your Facebook lead generation ads is essential to find out what works best for your audience. Neglecting ad testing can lead to stagnant campaigns that do not generate leads.

- Not Segmenting Leads

Segmenting your leads can help you to tailor your marketing messages to specific audiences, improving the chances of conversion. Neglecting lead segmentation can lead to generic messaging that fails to resonate with your audience.

In conclusion, Facebook lead generation campaigns require careful planning and execution to achieve success. Avoiding the above common mistakes can help you to create effective ad campaigns that generate leads and conversions. Remember to monitor your campaigns regularly, tweak where necessary, and optimize for the best results.

17

Scaling Your Facebook Lead Generation Efforts

As a digital marketer with years of experience, I can attest to the power of Facebook when it comes to lead generation. Facebook is the most popular social media platform, with over 2 billion active users, and it offers a range of tools and features that can help you scale your lead generation efforts.

Here are some key strategies for scaling your Facebook lead generation efforts:

1. Define your target audience: Before you start creating ads, it's important to define your target audience. This will help you create ads that resonate with your target market, and increase the likelihood of generating quality leads. Use Facebook's targeting options to select demographics, interests, behaviors, and more that align with your ideal customer.

2. Create a compelling offer: Your offer is what will entice people to click on your ad and fill out your lead form.

Make sure your offer is relevant, valuable, and irresistible. It could be a free trial, a discount, an ebook, or any other valuable content that speaks to your target audience.

3. Use high-quality visuals: Your ad visuals are the first thing people will see, so they need to be attention-grabbing and high-quality. Use clear and attractive images or videos that align with your brand and message.

4. Optimize your landing page: Your landing page is where people will land after clicking on your ad, so it needs to be optimized for conversions. Keep your landing page simple, visually appealing, and focused on your offer. Use a clear and concise headline, and make sure your lead form is easy to fill out.

5. Use retargeting: Retargeting is a powerful way to re-engage people who have interacted with your brand before. Use Facebook's retargeting options to show ads to people who have visited your website, engaged with your Facebook page, or taken some other action.

6. Test and optimize: Continuously test and optimize your ad campaigns to improve performance. Test different ad formats, targeting options, visuals, and copy to see what works best for your audience. Use Facebook's ad reporting tools to track your results and adjust your strategy accordingly.

7. Use automation tools: There are a variety of automation tools available that can help you scale your lead generation efforts on Facebook. For example, you can use chatbots to automate conversations with potential leads, or use lead management tools to streamline your lead nurturing process.

In conclusion, Facebook offers a wealth of opportunities for lead generation, and the key to success is to have a well-defined strategy, a compelling offer, and high-quality visuals. By following these strategies and continuously testing and optimizing your campaigns, you can scale your lead generation efforts and achieve your business goals.

18

Adapting Your Facebook Lead Generation Strategy to the Changing Landscape

As an experienced digital marketer, I can tell you that the Facebook landscape is constantly evolving, and it's essential to adapt your lead generation strategy to stay ahead of the curve. In recent years, Facebook has made significant changes to its algorithms and ad policies, making it more challenging to generate leads using traditional methods. However, with the right approach, you can still achieve great results.

Here are some tips on how to adapt your Facebook lead generation strategy to the changing landscape:

• Focus on Quality Over Quantity:

Gone are the days when you could generate leads by simply offering a free ebook or checklist in exchange for someone's email address. Facebook's algorithms are now geared towards showing users content that's relevant, valuable, and engaging. Therefore, it's more important than ever to focus on quality over quantity when it comes to lead generation.

Instead of creating generic lead magnets, try to offer something that's tailored to your target audience's specific needs and interests. For example, if you're targeting busy entrepreneurs, offer a free tool or template that helps them save time or improve productivity.

- Leverage Video Content:

Video content has become increasingly popular on Facebook in recent years, and for a good reason. Facebook's algorithms prioritize video content, making it more likely to appear in users' feeds. Additionally, video content tends to be more engaging and memorable than text-based content, making it an ideal format for lead generation.

Consider creating short, informative videos that highlight the benefits of your product or service. You can also create explainer videos that walk viewers through the sign-up process or offer a behind-the-scenes look at your business. Finally, consider using Facebook Live to host Q&A sessions or other events that allow you to engage with your audience in real-time.

- Use Lookalike Audiences:

Lookalike audiences are a powerful tool that allows you to target people who are similar to your existing customers. By using data from your website, email list, or Facebook page, Facebook can create a custom audience of people who share similar demographics, interests, and behaviors as your current customers.

Using lookalike audiences can be a highly effective way to reach new leads who are more likely to be interested in your product or service. However, it's essential to ensure that your targeting criteria are accurate to avoid wasting your ad spend on uninterested leads.

• Consider Messenger Ads:

Facebook Messenger has become a popular communication channel for businesses and consumers alike, with over 1.3 billion users worldwide. Messenger Ads are a relatively new ad format that allows you to connect with potential leads directly through Messenger.

Messenger Ads can be a highly effective way to generate leads because they allow you to engage with potential customers in a more personalized and conversational way. Consider using Messenger Ads to offer personalized recommendations, answer questions, or provide more information about your product or service.

• Test and Iterate:

Finally, it's crucial to test and iterate your lead generation strategy regularly. Facebook's algorithms and ad policies are continually changing, so what works today may not work tomorrow. By testing different ad formats, targeting criteria, and messaging, you can identify what works best for your business and optimize your strategy accordingly.

In conclusion, adapting your Facebook lead generation strategy to the changing landscape requires a combination of creativity, data analysis, and a willingness to experiment. By focusing on quality over quantity, leveraging video content, using lookalike audiences, considering Messenger Ads, and testing and iterating your strategy regularly, you can generate high-quality leads and stay ahead of the competition.

19

The Impact of Facebook Algorithm Changes on Lead Generation

As a digital marketer with extensive experience in lead generation, I can confidently say that Facebook algorithm changes have had a significant impact on the process. Over the years, Facebook has updated its algorithm numerous times, making it increasingly challenging for marketers to generate leads through the platform. In this article, we will explore the impact of Facebook algorithm changes on lead generation and how marketers can adapt their strategies to succeed in this evolving landscape.

Understanding Facebook Algorithm Changes

Facebook's algorithm is designed to prioritize content that is most relevant and engaging to users. In other words, Facebook wants users to see content that they are likely to interact with, whether it's through likes, comments, or shares. Over the years, Facebook has made several changes to its algorithm to improve the user experience, and these changes have had a significant impact on how businesses use the platform.

One of the most significant changes to the Facebook algorithm was made in 2018, when Facebook announced that it would prioritize content from family and friends over content from businesses and publishers. This change was a response to feedback from users who were concerned about the amount of branded content in their newsfeeds. As a result, businesses saw a significant decline in organic reach, making it harder to generate leads through Facebook.

Another significant change was made in 2021, when Facebook announced that it would start prioritizing content that users actively seek out and engage with. This means that businesses must create highly engaging content that resonates with their target audience if they want to appear in users' newsfeeds. This change makes it even more challenging for businesses to generate leads through the platform, as they must compete with other content creators for users' attention.

Impact of Facebook Algorithm Changes on Lead Generation

The impact of Facebook algorithm changes on lead generation has been significant. The decline in organic reach has made it harder for businesses to get their content in front of their target audience. As a result, businesses have had to invest more in paid advertising to reach their target audience, increasing the cost of lead generation.

Furthermore, Facebook's emphasis on user engagement means that businesses must create highly engaging content that resonates with their target audience. This requires a deep understanding of their audience's needs and interests, as well as the ability to create compelling content that stands out in a crowded marketplace.

How to Adapt to Facebook Algorithm Changes

To succeed in the current Facebook landscape, businesses must adapt their lead generation strategies to align with the platform's algorithm changes. Here are some strategies that businesses can use to generate leads through Facebook:

1. Invest in paid advertising: With the decline in organic reach, businesses must invest more in paid advertising to reach their target audience. This requires a solid understanding of Facebook's ad platform and the ability to create compelling ad copy and visuals.
2. Focus on user engagement: Businesses must create highly engaging content that resonates with their target audience. This requires a deep understanding of their audience's needs and interests, as well as the ability to create compelling content that stands out in a crowded marketplace.
3. Utilize Facebook groups: Facebook groups can be an excellent way to connect with your target audience and generate leads. By creating or joining groups that are relevant to your business, you can build relationships with potential customers and establish yourself as an authority in your industry.
4. Optimize your website for lead generation: While Facebook can be an excellent platform for generating leads, businesses should not rely solely on the platform. Instead, they should optimize their website for lead generation by creating compelling landing pages, offering valuable content in exchange for contact information, and using lead magnets to entice potential customers to take action.

In conclusion, the impact of Facebook algorithm changes on lead generation has been significant. However, businesses that are willing to adapt their strategies to align with these changes can still generate high-quality leads through the platform.

20

Combining Facebook and Instagram for Powerful Lead Generation

As a digital marketer with extensive experience in social media marketing, I can attest to the powerful combination of Facebook and Instagram for lead generation. Both platforms have a massive user base and offer robust advertising features that enable businesses to reach their target audience and generate quality leads. In this article, I will discuss the best practices for combining Facebook and Instagram to create a powerful lead generation strategy.

- Leverage Facebook Custom Audiences

Facebook Custom Audiences is a powerful tool that allows businesses to create targeted ads based on their existing customer database. By uploading email lists or phone numbers to Facebook, businesses can target their ads to their existing customers, which can be an effective way to generate leads. Additionally, Facebook Custom Audiences can also be used to create Lookalike Audiences, which are similar to your existing customers, but may not have interacted with your business yet. By targeting Lookalike Audiences, businesses can expand their reach and generate more leads.

• Use Instagram's Call-to-Action Buttons

Instagram offers several call-to-action (CTA) buttons that businesses can use to encourage users to take action, such as "Shop Now," "Learn More," and "Sign Up." By using these CTA buttons in your Instagram ads, you can drive traffic to your website and encourage users to sign up for your email list or newsletter, which can help generate leads.

• Create Engaging Visual Content

Both Facebook and Instagram are visual platforms, and businesses that create engaging visual content are more likely to generate leads. This can include eye-catching images, videos, and carousel ads that showcase your products or services. Additionally, businesses should consider using user-generated content, which can help build trust and credibility with potential customers.

• Use Facebook Lead Ads

Facebook Lead Ads are a type of ad that allows businesses to collect lead information directly within the Facebook platform. When users click on the ad, a lead form appears, which they can fill out without leaving Facebook. This can be an effective way to generate leads, as it removes the friction of navigating to a separate landing page.

- Re-target Website Visitors

Re-targeting is a powerful advertising strategy that involves targeting users who have already visited your website but did not convert. By re-targeting these users with Facebook and Instagram ads, businesses can remind them of their products or services and encourage them to take action, such as signing up for a newsletter or completing a lead form.

In conclusion, combining Facebook and Instagram for lead generation can be a powerful strategy for businesses. By leveraging Facebook Custom Audiences, Instagram's CTA buttons, creating engaging visual content, using Facebook Lead Ads, and re-targeting website visitors, businesses can generate quality leads and grow their business. However, it's important to remember that each platform has its unique audience and advertising features, and businesses should tailor their strategy accordingly.

21

The Power of Video in Facebook Lead Generation

A s a digital marketer with extensive experience in lead generation, I can confidently say that video is an incredibly powerful tool when it comes to generating leads on Facebook. Video content has been proven to be more engaging, memorable, and persuasive than other types of content, making it the perfect format for capturing the attention of potential customers and encouraging them to take action.

One of the primary advantages of using video in Facebook lead generation is that it allows you to convey complex ideas and emotions in a way that text and images simply cannot. Videos can demonstrate products in action, provide in-depth tutorials, or showcase customer success stories. By visually illustrating your brand's value proposition and showing your product or service in action, you can build trust and credibility with your audience and persuade them to take the next step in the customer journey.

Furthermore, Facebook's algorithm favors video content over other types of content, making it more likely that your video will appear in users' newsfeeds. By using video in your Facebook lead generation campaigns, you can increase the likelihood that your content will be seen by potential customers, which can ultimately lead to higher conversion rates.

Another advantage of using video in Facebook lead generation is that it can be used to retarget users who have already shown an interest in your brand. By using Facebook's retargeting capabilities, you can show personalized video ads to users who have interacted with your brand in some way, whether they have visited your website, engaged with your social media posts, or watched a previous video. This can help to keep your brand top of mind and encourage users to take the next step in the customer journey.

When it comes to creating effective video content for Facebook lead generation, there are several best practices to keep in mind. Firstly, it's important to keep your videos short and sweet, as attention spans on social media are notoriously short. Aim for videos that are between 15 and 60 seconds long, and make sure that your message is clear and concise.

Secondly, it's important to make sure that your videos are visually engaging and attention-grabbing. Use bright colors, bold graphics, and eye-catching animations to capture the attention of potential customers and keep them engaged throughout the video.

Finally, it's important to include a strong call-to-action (CTA) in your video. This could be a link to your website, an invitation to sign up for your email list, or a special offer for viewers who take action. By including a clear and compelling CTA, you can encourage viewers to take the next step in the customer journey and ultimately generate more leads for your business.

In conclusion, video is an incredibly powerful tool when

it comes to generating leads on Facebook. By using video content in your lead generation campaigns, you can build trust and credibility with your audience, increase your brand's visibility, and ultimately drive more conversions and sales for your business. So if you're not already using video in your Facebook lead generation strategy, now is the time to start!

22

Building Trust with Your Facebook Leads

As a digital marketer with years of experience, I understand the importance of building trust with Facebook leads. Trust is the foundation of any successful business relationship, and this holds true for your Facebook leads as well. When your leads trust you, they are more likely to convert into paying customers, and they will also refer their friends and family to your business. In this article, I will share with you some tips and strategies that will help you build trust with your Facebook leads.

- Provide Valuable Content

One of the best ways to build trust with your Facebook leads is by providing them with valuable content. This can include blog posts, infographics, videos, and webinars that educate your audience about your products and services. When you provide your leads with valuable content, they will see you as an authority in your industry, and they will be more likely to trust you.

- Respond Quickly

Another important factor in building trust with your Facebook leads is responding to their inquiries quickly. When a lead reaches out to you with a question or concern, make sure that you respond promptly. This shows that you value their time and are committed to providing excellent customer service.

- Be Transparent

Transparency is key to building trust with your Facebook leads. Make sure that your Facebook page includes all relevant information about your business, including your contact information, hours of operation, and any other important details. If you make a mistake or experience an issue, be honest and transparent with your leads. This will show that you are committed to accountability and will help you build trust over time.

- Use Social Proof

Social proof is another powerful tool for building trust with your Facebook leads. This can include customer reviews, testimonials, and case studies that showcase the positive experiences that others have had with your business. When your leads see that others have had a positive experience with your business, they will be more likely to trust you as well.

- Engage with Your Audience

Engaging with your Facebook audience is another important way to build trust. This can include responding to comments, participating in discussions, and sharing relevant content. When you engage with your audience, you show that you care about their opinions and are committed to building a relationship with them.

- Personalize Your Communication

Finally, personalizing your communication with your Facebook leads can help build trust. Use their name when responding to comments or messages, and personalize your content to their interests and needs. When your leads feel like you are speaking directly to them, they will be more likely to trust you.

In conclusion, building trust with your Facebook leads is essential for the success of your business. By providing valuable content, responding quickly, being transparent, using social proof, engaging with your audience, and personalizing your communication, you can establish a strong foundation of trust with your leads. With time and consistency, this trust will translate into increased conversions, customer loyalty, and long-term success.

23

Using Social Proof to Boost Facebook Lead Generation

Social proof is a powerful psychological phenomenon that can be leveraged by digital marketers to increase lead generation on Facebook. Social proof refers to the tendency for people to conform to the behavior of others in their social circle or community. By demonstrating that others have taken a particular action, such as signing up for a service or purchasing a product, social proof can encourage others to follow suit.

In the context of Facebook lead generation, social proof can be used to demonstrate to potential leads that others have already taken the desired action of signing up for a newsletter or filling out a contact form. This can increase the perceived value of the offer and create a sense of urgency to act.

Here are some effective strategies for using social proof to boost Facebook lead generation:

- Display social proof on your Facebook page

One way to leverage social proof is by displaying the number of likes, followers, and shares on your Facebook page. This can help demonstrate to potential leads that your brand has a strong social presence and a loyal following. You can also showcase testimonials or reviews from satisfied customers to demonstrate the value of your offering.

- Use social proof in your Facebook ads

Another effective strategy is to use social proof in your Facebook ads. This can be done by displaying customer reviews or ratings, highlighting the number of people who have already signed up for your offer, or showcasing a celebrity endorsement. By including social proof in your ad copy or imagery, you can increase the perceived value of your offer and create a sense of urgency to act.

- Leverage user-generated content

User-generated content (UGC) is another powerful form of social proof. By featuring UGC on your Facebook page or in your ads, you can demonstrate that others have already engaged with your brand or offering. This can include photos, videos, or reviews from satisfied customers. UGC can be particularly effective in industries such as fashion, travel, or food, where visuals can have a strong impact on consumer behavior.

- Create a sense of FOMO (fear of missing out)

Creating a sense of FOMO is another effective way to leverage social proof to boost Facebook lead generation. This can be done by highlighting limited-time offers, showcasing the number of people who have already signed up, or creating a sense of exclusivity around your offer. By creating a sense of urgency or scarcity, you can encourage potential leads to take action and sign up for your offer.

In conclusion, social proof is a powerful psychological phenomenon that can be leveraged by digital marketers to increase lead generation on Facebook. By displaying social proof on your Facebook page, using social proof in your Facebook ads, leveraging user-generated content, and creating a sense of FOMO, you can increase the perceived value of your offer and create a sense of urgency to act. With these strategies in mind, you can boost your Facebook lead generation and achieve your marketing goals.

24

Integrating Facebook Lead Generation with Your Sales Strategy

As a digital marketer with years of experience, I understand the importance of generating quality leads for any business to succeed. Facebook has become a valuable platform for lead generation due to its massive user base and advanced targeting capabilities. Integrating Facebook lead generation with your sales strategy can help you increase your sales and grow your business. In this article, I will discuss the steps involved in integrating Facebook lead generation with your sales strategy.

1. Define your target audience: The first step in integrating Facebook lead generation with your sales strategy is to define your target audience. Facebook offers a wide range of targeting options that allow you to reach specific groups of people based on demographics, interests, behaviors, and more. Defining your target audience will help you create more effective ads that resonate with your ideal customer.
2. Create a lead magnet: A lead magnet is a free resource

or incentive that you offer to your target audience in exchange for their contact information. It can be anything from an e-book, whitepaper, or webinar to a discount or free trial. The key is to offer something of value that your target audience wants.

3. Create a lead generation ad: Once you have defined your target audience and created a lead magnet, it's time to create a lead generation ad. A lead generation ad is a type of Facebook ad that allows people to submit their contact information directly within the ad itself, without leaving Facebook. This makes it easy for people to sign up for your offer, which can help increase your conversion rates.

4. Set up a lead capture form: When someone submits their contact information through your lead generation ad, you need to have a system in place to capture and store that information. Facebook offers a built-in lead capture form that you can use, or you can integrate your own form with a third-party provider.

5. Follow up with your leads: Once you have captured your leads' contact information, it's important to follow up with them promptly. You can set up automated email sequences or phone calls to nurture your leads and move them through your sales funnel.

6. Measure your results: Like any marketing campaign, it's important to measure your results to see how effective your Facebook lead generation strategy is. Facebook provides detailed metrics on the performance of your ads, including the number of leads generated, cost per lead, and conversion rates. Use this data to optimize your campaigns and improve your results over time.

Integrating Facebook lead generation with your sales strategy can help you reach your target audience, generate quality leads, and increase your sales. By following these steps and continually optimizing your campaigns, you can create a highly effective lead generation machine that drives growth for your business.

25

Future Trends in Facebook Lead Generation.

As an experienced digital marketer, I have observed the evolution of Facebook as a key player in the digital marketing world. Over the years, Facebook has transformed from a social media platform to a powerful marketing tool for businesses of all sizes. One of the most critical aspects of Facebook marketing is lead generation. However, the techniques used for lead generation on Facebook are constantly changing. In this article, I will discuss some of the future trends in Facebook lead generation that every digital marketer should be aware of.

1. Personalization will be key: Personalization has been a buzzword in the marketing industry for some time now, and it will continue to play a critical role in lead generation on Facebook. With the vast amount of data available on Facebook, marketers can create personalized campaigns that resonate with their target audience. By using data such as interests, behaviors, and demographics, marketers

can create tailored ads that are more likely to convert leads into customers.

2. Video content will dominate: Video content has been gaining traction on Facebook, and this trend is set to continue. In fact, recent studies show that video content on Facebook generates more engagement than any other type of content. Marketers should leverage this trend by creating video ads that capture the attention of their target audience. These videos should be short, engaging, and visually appealing.

3. Chatbots will become more prevalent: Chatbots are becoming increasingly popular in the marketing industry, and they will play a significant role in Facebook lead generation in the future. By using chatbots, marketers can engage with their target audience in real-time and provide them with personalized recommendations. Chatbots can also be used to qualify leads, which can help businesses save time and resources.

4. Augmented Reality (AR) will be the next big thing: Augmented Reality is a technology that overlays digital information onto the real world, and it has the potential to revolutionize Facebook lead generation. With AR, marketers can create immersive experiences that allow users to interact with their products or services in real-time. For example, a furniture store could use AR to show customers how a piece of furniture would look in their home before they make a purchase.

5. Facebook Groups will become more important: Facebook Groups have been around for a while, but they are becoming increasingly important for lead generation. By creating and participating in Facebook Groups, marketers can

engage with their target audience and build relationships with potential customers. Facebook Groups can also be used to collect feedback from customers, which can help businesses improve their products and services.

In conclusion, Facebook lead generation is an ever-evolving field, and it is important for digital marketers to stay up-to-date with the latest trends. Personalization, video content, chatbots, augmented reality, and Facebook Groups are all trends that are set to shape the future of Facebook lead generation. By leveraging these trends, marketers can create effective campaigns that generate high-quality leads and drive business growth.

26

Why having followers for your page only from your target audience or similar followers is vital

As a seasoned digital marketer, I can confidently say that having followers for your page only from your target audience or similar followers is crucial for the success of your marketing efforts. Let me explain why.

Firstly, your target audience is the group of people who are most likely to be interested in your product or service. They are the ones who are more likely to engage with your content, make a purchase, or become loyal customers. Therefore, having followers from your target audience ensures that you are reaching the right people and that your content is resonating with the people who are most likely to convert.

On the other hand, having followers who are not part of your target audience can be detrimental to your marketing efforts. These followers may not be interested in your product or service, and as a result, they are unlikely to engage with your content or make a purchase. Furthermore, having a large number of followers who are not part of your target audience can skew your engagement metrics and make it difficult to determine the success of your marketing campaigns.

Secondly, having followers from similar pages or accounts is essential because it helps you to expand your reach to people who are interested in the same or related topics. For example, if you are a fashion brand, having followers from other fashion-related pages or accounts can expose your brand to a new audience that is already interested in fashion. These followers are more likely to engage with your content and become loyal customers.

Moreover, having followers from similar pages or accounts can also help you to build relationships with other brands or businesses in your industry. By engaging with their followers and collaborating on marketing campaigns, you can create a mutually beneficial relationship that can lead to increased brand exposure and revenue.

In conclusion, having followers for your page only from your target audience or similar followers is vital for the success of your marketing efforts. By reaching the right people and expanding your reach to people who are interested in the same or related topics, you can increase your engagement metrics and build a loyal customer base. So, if you are looking to grow your brand and increase your revenue, focus on attracting followers who are part of your target audience or similar followers.

27

How to gain followers for your page only from your target audience or similar followers

As a digital marketer with years of experience, I understand that gaining followers for your page can be a daunting task. It's not just about the numbers; it's about getting the right people to follow you - your target audience or similar followers. This is because the right followers can help you build a loyal and engaged community, drive more traffic to your website, and ultimately increase your business's revenue. In this article, I will share some proven strategies that can help you gain followers from your target audience or similar followers.

- Define your target audience

The first step to gaining followers from your target audience is to define who they are. You need to understand their demographics, interests, and online behavior. You can use tools like Google Analytics, Facebook Insights, or Twitter Analytics to gain insights into your current followers' characteristics. Once you have a good understanding of your target audience, you can tailor your content to meet their needs and preferences.

• Use hashtags strategically

Hashtags are a great way to get your content in front of your target audience. You can use relevant hashtags in your posts, stories, and reels to increase your visibility. Make sure you use popular hashtags that your target audience is likely to search for. You can also create your own branded hashtag and encourage your followers to use it in their posts.

• Collaborate with influencers

Influencer marketing is a powerful way to reach your target audience. You can collaborate with influencers who have a similar audience to yours and ask them to promote your page to their followers. This can help you gain new followers who are interested in your niche.

• Run targeted ads

Social media advertising allows you to target specific audiences based on their interests, demographics, and behavior. You can use this to your advantage by running targeted ads to reach your ideal followers. Make sure your ad copy and visuals are compelling and relevant to your target audience.

• Engage with your followers

Engaging with your followers is key to building a loyal and engaged community. Respond to their comments, DMs, and mentions promptly. Ask for their feedback, opinions, and suggestions. You can also run polls, quizzes, and contests to encourage engagement and increase your reach.

• Share user-generated content

User-generated content (UGC) is content created by your followers or customers. Sharing UGC can help you build social proof and encourage more people to follow you. Make sure you ask for permission before sharing UGC and give proper credit to the original creator.

• Optimize your profile

Your social media profile is the first thing your potential followers will see. Make sure it's optimized for your target audience. Use a clear and professional profile picture, write a compelling bio, and include relevant keywords. You can also add a call-to-action (CTA) to your profile to encourage people to follow you.

• Post consistently

Consistency is key when it comes to social media marketing. You need to post regularly to stay top-of-mind with your followers and attract new ones. Create a content calendar and schedule your posts in advance. Make sure your content is high-quality, relevant, and engaging.

• Monitor your metrics

Finally, you need to monitor your social media metrics to see what's working and what's not. Use tools like Google Analytics, Facebook Insights, or Twitter Analytics to track your follower growth, engagement, and reach. Analyze your data regularly and adjust your strategy accordingly.

In conclusion, gaining followers from your target audience or similar followers requires a strategic approach. You need to define your target audience, use hashtags strategically, collaborate with influencers, run targeted ads, engage with your followers, share user-generated content, optimize your profile, post consistently, and monitor your metrics.

28

How to write effective facebook ad copies and tools to speed up this process

As a digital marketer, writing effective Facebook ad copies is an essential skill that can help you attract the attention of your target audience, drive engagement, and increase your conversion rates. Crafting an effective ad copy involves understanding your target audience, being clear and concise in your messaging, and utilizing persuasive language that resonates with your audience.

In this article, I will provide you with some tips on how to write effective Facebook ad copies and the tools that can help you speed up this process.

Understanding Your Target Audience

The first step in writing an effective Facebook ad copy is to understand your target audience. You need to identify who your target audience is and what they are looking for in your product or service. Knowing your target audience will help you craft an ad copy that resonates with them and motivates them to take action.

To understand your target audience, you can use Facebook's Audience Insights tool. This tool helps you to analyze your audience demographics, interests, and behaviors. You can use this information to tailor your ad copy to your target audience and increase the chances of them engaging with your ad.

Being Clear and Concise

The next step is to be clear and concise in your messaging. Your ad copy should communicate the benefits of your product or service in a clear and concise manner. It should be easy to read and understand, and it should convey the value proposition of your product or service.

To be clear and concise, you can follow these tips:

- Use simple language and avoid using jargon or technical terms.
- Focus on the benefits of your product or service, rather than its features.
- Use bullet points or short paragraphs to break up your text and make it easier to read.

Utilizing Persuasive Language

The final step is to utilize persuasive language that resonates with your audience. Persuasive language can motivate your audience to take action and increase the chances of them converting. Some examples of persuasive language include:

- Urgency: Use phrases such as "limited time offer" or "while supplies last" to create a sense of urgency.
- Exclusivity: Use phrases such as "exclusive offer" or "limited edition" to create a sense of exclusivity.

- Social Proof: Use customer testimonials or reviews to demonstrate social proof and increase the credibility of your product or service.

Tools to Speed up the Ad Copywriting Process

Now that you understand the key elements of an effective Facebook ad copy, let's take a look at some tools that can help you speed up the ad copywriting process.

- Copy.ai

Copy.ai is an AI-powered tool that can help you generate ad copy in minutes. This tool uses machine learning algorithms to analyze your target audience and generate ad copy that resonates with them. All you have to do is enter some basic information about your product or service, and Copy.ai will generate ad copy that you can use in your Facebook ads.

- Grammarly

Grammarly is a tool that can help you improve the grammar and clarity of your ad copy. This tool checks your ad copy for spelling and grammar errors, as well as clarity and conciseness. It can also suggest alternative phrasing or sentence structure to make your ad copy more effective.

- Canva

Canva is a graphic design tool that can help you create eye-catching visuals for your Facebook ads. This tool provides a wide range of templates and design elements that you can use to create high-quality graphics for your ads. Canva also has a library of stock images and icons that you can use to enhance your ad visuals.

- Facebook Ads Manager

Facebook Ads Manager is a tool that can help you create and manage your Facebook ad campaigns. This tool provides you with a range of targeting options and ad formats that you can use to reach your target audience.

29

Scheduling posts and ways to optimize your reach organically in Facebook

As a digital marketer, I understand the importance of scheduling social media posts in advance to optimize reach and engagement. Facebook, being the most popular social media platform, requires a well-planned approach to maximize organic reach. In this article, I'll share my experience and expertise on scheduling posts and ways to optimize reach organically on Facebook.

Scheduling Posts on Facebook Facebook's scheduling feature allows you to schedule your posts in advance, giving you the freedom to focus on other aspects of your social media strategy. To schedule a post, follow these simple steps:

Step 1: Create a post Step 2: Click on the arrow next to the "Publish" button Step 3: Select "Schedule" Step 4: Choose the date and time you want the post to go live Step 5: Click on "Schedule"

Once scheduled, your post will appear in your Facebook Page's "Scheduled Posts" section, where you can make changes or delete the post if necessary.

Ways to Optimize Reach Organically on Facebook Organic reach on Facebook has declined in recent years, making it challenging to reach your target audience without paid advertising. However, there are still ways to optimize your reach organically. Here are some effective strategies:

1. Share Engaging Content The content you share on Facebook should be relevant, interesting, and engaging to your audience. High-quality content that adds value to your followers is more likely to be shared, which can increase your reach organically.

2. Use Visuals Visuals, such as images and videos, are more likely to grab attention and generate engagement than text-only posts. Use high-quality visuals that are relevant to your content to maximize their impact.

3. Use Hashtags Hashtags are a great way to increase your post's visibility on Facebook. Use relevant hashtags that relate to your post and target audience to increase your reach organically.

4. Post at Optimal Times Knowing when your audience is most active on Facebook is crucial to optimizing your reach. Posting at optimal times ensures that your content is seen by the maximum number of people. Use Facebook Insights to track the performance of your posts and identify the best times to post.

5. Encourage Engagement Encouraging engagement on your posts is an effective way to increase reach organically. Ask questions, start conversations, and respond to comments to encourage engagement and increase the visibility of your posts.

6. Share User-Generated Content Sharing user-generated

content on your Facebook page is an excellent way to increase reach organically. User-generated content is content created by your followers and can include reviews, testimonials, and photos. Sharing this content shows that you value your followers and can increase engagement and reach.

7. Utilize Facebook Groups Facebook groups are an excellent way to reach a targeted audience and increase engagement. Join relevant groups and share your content with members to increase your reach organically. Make sure to follow group rules and engage with other members to build relationships and credibility.

8. Use Facebook Live Facebook Live is a powerful tool that can increase engagement and reach organically. Live video generates six times more engagement than regular video and allows you to connect with your audience in real-time. Use Facebook Live to share valuable content, host Q&A sessions, or showcase your products or services.

In conclusion, scheduling posts and optimizing reach organically on Facebook requires a strategic approach. By creating engaging content, using visuals, hashtags, and posting at optimal times, encouraging engagement, sharing user-generated content, utilizing Facebook groups, and using Facebook Live, you can increase your reach organically and connect with your target audience effectively. With consistent effort and experimentation, you can build a successful social media strategy that drives engagement, conversions, and brand awareness.

30

Top free tools to increase effective Facebook lead generation results

A s a digital marketer with extensive experience in Facebook lead generation, I can attest to the fact that the success of any lead generation campaign on this platform depends on the tools used. In this era of technological advancements, there are several free tools available that can help you generate effective leads on Facebook. Here are the top free tools you can use to increase your Facebook lead generation results.

• Facebook Lead Ads

Facebook Lead Ads is one of the most effective tools for generating leads on the platform. This tool allows businesses to create lead generation forms that capture user data, such as name, email address, and phone number, without users having to leave Facebook. This means that users can quickly fill out the form without the hassle of going to an external landing page.

With Facebook Lead Ads, you can target your audience based

on their demographics, interests, and behaviors, ensuring that your ads are shown to the right people. Additionally, Facebook Lead Ads can integrate with your customer relationship management (CRM) tool, enabling you to manage your leads and follow up with them effectively.

• Facebook Pixel

Facebook Pixel is a powerful tool that helps you track and measure the effectiveness of your Facebook ads. It is a small piece of code that you place on your website, and it allows you to track user behavior on your site after they have clicked on your Facebook ad.

With Facebook Pixel, you can track how many people clicked on your ad and then performed the desired action, such as filling out a lead generation form. This data can help you optimize your Facebook ads and landing pages to increase your lead generation results.

• Canva

Canva is a free graphic design tool that allows you to create visually appealing graphics for your Facebook ads and landing pages. With Canva, you can create professional-looking graphics without any design skills.

Canva offers a wide range of templates, images, and graphics that you can use to create your ads and landing pages. You can also customize these templates to suit your brand's needs. By creating visually appealing graphics, you can capture the attention of your audience and increase the likelihood of them filling out your lead generation form.

- Hootsuite

Hootsuite is a social media management tool that allows you to manage all your social media accounts, including Facebook, from one platform. With Hootsuite, you can schedule your Facebook posts, monitor your social media mentions, and track your social media analytics.

By scheduling your Facebook posts, you can ensure that your content is posted at the optimal time for your audience, increasing the chances of your posts being seen by your target audience. Additionally, by monitoring your social media mentions, you can engage with your audience and build relationships with potential leads.

- Facebook Audience Insights

Facebook Audience Insights is a tool that allows you to gather data on your target audience. With this tool, you can get insights into your audience's demographics, interests, behaviors, and more.

By understanding your target audience, you can create more targeted Facebook ads that resonate with them, increasing the likelihood of them filling out your lead generation form. Additionally, by analyzing your audience data, you can make data-driven decisions and optimize your lead generation campaigns for better results.

- Google Analytics

Google Analytics is a free web analytics tool that allows you to track your website's performance. With Google Analytics, you can track your website traffic, user behavior, and conversion rates.

By analyzing your website data, you can gain insights into how users interact with your website and optimize your website for better lead generation results. Additionally, by tracking your conversion rates, you can identify areas for improvement and make data-driven decisions to increase your lead generation results.

In conclusion, Facebook lead generation can be challenging, but with the right tools, it can be a rewarding experience.

www.ingramcontent.com/pod-product-compliance
Lightning Source LLC
Chambersburg PA
CBHW070435220526
45466CB00004B/1690